THE
SUGARLESS COOKBOOK

No sugar — No honey

Over 80% without
artificial sweeteners

BY:

Addie Gonshorowski

ACKNOWLEDGEMENT

Special thanks to my family
for their constant support
and patience. Also, to Eleanor
Latterell, Registered Dietitian
for evaluation of ** marked
recipes.

PUBLISHED BY

ADDIE'S RECIPE BOX
DRAWER 5426-SL80
EUGENE, OREGON 97405

TO

MY DAUGHTERS

Carolyn & Toni Marie

FOREWARD

The recipes are intended to help add a variety to your diet without the use of sugar, honey or artificial sweeteners.

Most of the recipes are made without sweetners with the exception of jams, Ice cream & a few desserts & salads.

To give more variety, sweeteners have been used in a few recipes since many people do not object to their use and like to make jams, Ice cream etc.

Once you get used to foods without a lot of sweetener you may find that the food is just as enjoyable and in many cases more so then sweetened ones.

For those of you who prefer a sweeter taste then can be gotten by using only natural ingredients, then by all means add a little sweetener.

For those of you that can have sugar or honey, just add a little to the recipe.

Relatively few cookbooks have been published without the sugar, honey or artificial sweeteners, therefore, I am pleased to be able to offer my recipes in this book.

I hope you will enjoy this way of preparing foods as much as I and my family have.

Addie Gonshorowski

NOTICE

The recipes in this book have been carefully selected to avoid ingredients that may not be allowed in most diets.

These recipes do not contain any sugar or honey and therefore, should be adaptable to most sugar restricted diets.

Each recipe should be checked with your diet allowance before using.

THE AUTHOR is not responsible for ingredients listed that are not allowed in an individuals diet.

It is recommended that you discuss with your diet counselor any recipes used, and if on a strict diet to calculate all calories and exchanges as the ones listed are approximated.

The author is not responsible for any calories or exchanges that are not exact as these are approximate figures and should be regarded as such.

It is up to each individual to follow your own diet and to check ingredients, calories, and exchanges according to your allowances.

Avoid any recipes that contain ingredients not allowed unless you can substitute or eliminate that ingredient.

AUTHOR NOT LIABLE for anything beyond the price of one book.

CONTENTS

****

NOTICE

Author and/or publisher not responsible
for anything beyond the price of one
book.

HOW TO WARM FOODS

For cakes, cookies & tea breads - wrap in
foil and place in hot oven for few minutes
or until warm.

HOW TO MAKE ICE WATER

Fill bowl with crushed ice. ADD water and
let set for few minutes.

Drain amount of water needed.

KEEP FOODS REFRIGERATED

Foods made with artificial sweeteners must
be kept refrigerated and used within a few
days.

If food is to be kept for more than a few
days it is advisable to freeze if possible.

CALORIE INFORMATION

To cut calories Diet margarine can be used
in place of regular margarine in recipes
that call for margarine. Diet margarine
contains about 1/2 the calories of regular.
So if desired you may substitute.

SWEETENERS

There are many different kinds of sweeteners
on the market today... It is impossible to
know all products available in different
areas...

Use your favorite sweetener but be sure to
note if it contains any calories or restrict-
ions on the package and allow for them in
your diet.

BREADS, MUFFINS

PRUNE ROLLS

1 loaf frozen unbaked bread
12 prunes, pitted, cooked & mashed
1/4 tsp lemon juice (optional)
1/2 tsp cinnamon

****

SLICE frozen unbaked bread into 12
slices.

LET thaw out and flatten and stretch
out enough to hold filling.

FILLING:

MIX prunes, lemon juice & cinnamon.

DIVIDE between rolls evenly; Fold up
corners and seal well.

PLACE upside down in greased muffin pans.

LET rise to double.

BAKE 350 degrees about 20 minutes or
to nicely browned.

TURN out on rack to cool

BEST eaten first day or warmed slightly.

APPROXIMATE EXCHANGE - 1/12 of recipe =

1 bread - 1/2 fruit

BANANA BREAD

2 small bananas
2 medium eggs
1/2 cup shortening
12 dates, Soaked 5 minutes, Drain & chop.
1-3/4 cup flour
2 tsp baking powder
1 tsp soda
1/2 tsp salt
1 tsp cinnamon
12 small walnuts, chopped

****

CUT UP banana and beat to a liquid.

ADD eggs and beat well.

CREAM shortening and add to banana
mixture; Add dates.

MIX flour, baking powder, soda, salt,
cinnamon and nuts.

STIR into creamed mixture just enough
to moisten. (Do not beat)

BAKE in 5 X 9" greased loaf pan 325
degrees 45 to 60 minutes to done.

SERVE slightly warm

APPROXIMATE EXCHANGE: 1/24 th of recipe =

1/2 bread - 1/2 fruit - trace meat - 1 fat

PARSNIP BANANA BREAD

1/3 cup parsnips, mashed
1 small banana
2 medium eggs
1/2 cup shortening
1-3/4 cup flour
1 tsp cinnamon
2 tsp baking powder
1 tsp soda
1/2 tsp salt
12 dates, Soak 5 minutes; Drain & chop.
12 small walnuts, chopped

****

COOK peeled parsnip in 1/2 cup apple juice
about 45 minutes to tender; Drain and
mash; Then measure 1/3 cup.

CUT up banana; Add parsnips and beat to
a liquid. Add creamed shortening & beat.

ADD slightly beaten eggs and mix.

MIX flour, cinnamon, baking powder,
soda and salt.

STIR into creamed mixture just to moisten.

FOLD in dates and nuts.

BAKE in 5 X 9" greased loaf pan 325
degrees about 45 minutes to 1 hour.. Test
with tooth pick.

APPROXIMATE EXCHANGE: 1/24 =

1/2 bread - 1/3 fruit - 1-1/10 fat

APPLESAUCE BREAD

1/2 cup margarine	1 tsp soda
2 eggs	1 tsp salt
1 tsp vanilla	2 tsp cinnamon
2 cups flour	1/2 tsp nutmeg
1 tsp baking powder	1 cup raisins

1 cup unsweetened applesauce
18 small walnuts, chopped fine

****

CREAM margarine; Add eggs and vanilla
and beat well.

COMBINE flour, baking powder, soda, salt,
cinnamon and nutmeg.

ADD flour and applesauce alternately to
creamed mixture and mix well.

ADD raisins and nuts.

POUR into greased loaf pan and let stand
20 minutes.

BAKE 350 degrees about 1 hour or until
done.

SERVE slightly warm slices with little
butter if desired.

EXCHANGE:

1/12 of recipe = 1 bread - 3/4 fruit -
2-1/3 fat - 1/6 meat

(For fluffy raisins - Soak in hot water
  5 minutes then drain well before adding)

CARROT PRUNE BREAD

3/4 cup salad oil
2 eggs
1-1/2 cups grated raw carrots
1-1/2 cup flour
2 tsp cinnamon
1 tsp salt
1 tsp soda
1/2 cup prunes (about 14)

****

MIX oil and slightly beaten egg until well blended.

STIR in carrots and cooked, chopped prunes.

MIX together flour, cinnamon, salt and soda.

ADD to creamed mixture whipping in well with a fork.

POUR into greased loaf pan 9" X 5" and bake 350 degrees about 60 to 65 minutes or until done.

REMOVE from oven and let set 5 minutes in pan; Turn out on rack to cool.

SERVE slightly warmed slices.

EXCHANGE:

1/12 of recipe = 3/4 bread - 2/3 fruit - 1/6 meat - 1/4 #2 vegetable - 3 fat

RAISIN BREAD

1/4 cup margarine, melted
1 cup buttermilk, skim
3 tsp baking powder
24 small walnuts, chopped
2 tsp cinnamon
3/4 cup raisins, chopped
1 small apple, peeled & fine chopped

2 eggs medium
2 cups flour
1/4 tsp salt
1/2 tsp soda

****

BEAT eggs and add buttermilk and margarine.

MIX flour, baking powder, salt, soda,
cinnamon, walnuts, raisins, & apple.

COMBINE the two mixtures and mix just
enough to combine ingredients.

BAKE in greased loaf pan 5 X 9" in a 350
degree oven for about 50 to 60 minutes.

COOL on rack 10 minutes. Turn out of pan.

SERVE slightly warm slices.

APPROXIMATE EXCHANGE - 1/24 of recipe =

1/2 bread, 1/3 fruit, 2/3 fat, trace milk
trace meat

* *

APPLE BREAD

2 tblsp cooking oil	1 egg, medium
1 tsp baking powder	1 cup flour
1 tsp cinnamon	1/4 tsp soda
3 tblsp Orange juice	1/4 tsp salt
1 small apple	1/2 cup raisins

****

BEAT egg with cooking oil.

MIX flour, baking powder, cinnamon, soda, salt,

SOAK raisins in hot water 5 minutes. DRAIN.

ADD a little flour mixture to oil & mix just to blend.

ADD the orange juice and rest of flour.

STIR just enough to moisten.

ADD peeled chopped apple and raisins.

BAKE in small (3½ X 7½") loaf pan at 350 degrees about 45 minutes to done.

MAKES 13 slices. SERVE slightly warm.

APPROXIMATE EXCHANGE - 1/13 of recipe =

1/2 bread, 1/3 fruit, 1/2 fat, trace meat

**

CARROT BREAD

1 cup raw carrots	1 cup flour
1 tsp baking powder	3/4 tsp soda
1-1/2 tsp cinnamon	1/4 tsp salt
1/4 cup cooking oil	1 egg, medium
1/2 cup raisins	1 tblsp water

****

MIX TOGETHER flour, baking powder, soda, cinnamon, salt

GRIND carrots on medium fine setting.

COMBINE oil, eggs & water. BEAT.

ADD flour mixture to egg mixture & stir just to moisten.

ADD carrots & raisins.

BAKE in small (3½ X 7½") greased loaf pan 350 degrees about 40 to 45 minutes.

SERVE slightly warm.

APPROXIMATE EXCHANGE - 1/12 of recipe =

1/2 bread, 2/3 fruit, 1/12 meat, 1/6 "B" veg, 1 fat

**

BANANA NUT MUFFINS

1 egg
1 small banana, mashed
1 tsp vanilla
2 tsp water
1-1/3 cup cake flour
1/2 tsp salt
3 tsp baking powder
1 tsp cinnamon
2/3 cup skim milk
2 tblsp shortening, melted
1/2 cup currants
20 small walnuts, chopped

****

BEAT egg; Add banana, vanilla & water.

MIX flour, salt, baking powder, cinnamon together.

ADD alternately with milk to banana mixture.

SOAK currants in hot water & drain well.

ADD currants, shortening and nuts & mix well.

FILL greased small muffin pans 3/4 full and bake 400 degrees about 20 minutes.

SERVE warm with little butter.

EXCHANGE: 1/12 recipe = 3/4 bread - 1/2 fruit - trace meat - trace milk - 3/4 fat

BANANA BRAN MUFFINS

1 cup flour, sifted	1 egg, beaten
2½ tsp baking powder	1/4 cup skim milk
1/2 tsp salt	2 tblsp oil
1½ tsp cinnamon	1/2 cup currants
1 cup whole bran cereal	
2 small ripe bananas, mashed	

****

MIX flour, baking powder and salt & cinnamon & bran.

COMBINE egg, bananas, currants, milk & oil.

MAKE a well in center of dry ingredients and add liquids all at once.

STIR just to moisten.

FILL well greased muffin pans 2/3 full.

BAKE 400 degrees 15 minutes or until done.

SERVE at once or warm later.

EXCHANGE: COMPLETE RECIPE = 7-3/4 bread
1/4 milk - 8 fruit - 1 meat - 6½ fat

(Divide by number of muffins you make to
  determine exchange in each)

DATE NUT MUFFINS

2 tblsp margarine, melted   1 egg, medium
1/2 cup skim buttermilk   1 cup flour
1½ tsp baking powder   1/8 tsp salt
1 tsp cinnamon   1/4 tsp soda
12 dates, chopped fine
9 small walnuts, chopped

****

BEAT egg, Add margarine & buttermilk.

MIX flour, baking powder, salt, soda,
walnuts, cinnamon & dates.

ADD to egg mixture & stir just to blend.

BAKE in greased muffin pans 350 degrees
about 20 minutes or until done.

APPROXIMATE EXCHANGE - 1/12 of recipe =

1/2 bread, trace milk, 1/2 fruit, 2/3
fat, 1/12 meat.

SERVE slightly warm

CAKES

SWEET POTATO CAKE

2/3 cup margarine
1 cup sweet potatoes
    cooked & mashed
4 eggs, separated
1 tsp vanilla
2 cups cake flour
2 tsp pumpkin pie spice

4 tsp cocoa
1 tblsp baking
         powder
1/2 tsp soda
1/2 tsp salt
3/4 cup skim milk
1/2 cup raisins

18 small chopped pecans

****

CREAM margarine; Add sweet potatoes; Beat
in egg yolks and vanilla.

MIX together 1-1/2 cup cake flour, spice,
cocoa, baking powder, soda & salt.

ADD to creamed mixture alternately with
milk.

SPRINKLE 1/2 cup flour over raisins and
nuts; Then add to mixture.

BEAT egg whites to stiff and fold in
to mixture carefully.

BAKE in greased and floured 9 X 13"
baking pan 350 degrees about 40 to 60
minutes or until done.

SERVE slightly warm with little Ice
cream from your allowance.

APPROXIMATE EXCHANGE: 1/24th of recipe =

3/4 bread - 1/5 fruit - 1/6 meat - 3/4 fat.

DATE NUT CAKE

1/2 cup margarine, Very soft
2 eggs, room temperature
1 tsp vanilla
1/2 tsp cinnamon
1/4 tsp cloves
1 tblsp cocoa
2 cups self-rising flour
2 tsp baking powder
32 dates,
20 small walnuts, chopped
1-1/2 cup unsweetened applesauce

****

MIX margarine, eggs & vanilla until
creamy.

MIX cinnamon, cocoa, flour, baking powder
together.

ADD applesauce to egg mixture.

SOAK dates in hot water 5 minutes and
cut up with scissors.

STIR in flour mixture.. Fold in dates
and nuts.

BAKE in 8" X 8" lightly greased pan 350
degrees about 45 minutes to done.

EXCHANGE: 25 servings; Each serving =

1/2 bread - 3/4 fruit - 1-1/5 fat

CINNAMON CAKE

1 cup + 3 tblsp cake flour
    (sift before measure)
1-1/2 tsp baking powder
1/2 tsp salt
1 tsp cinnamon
1 tsp vanilla
1/4 cup oil
3 egg yolks
1/3 cup water
4 whites of egg
1/4 tsp cream tartar

****

MIX dry ingredients. MAKE a well in center and add vanilla, oil, yolks & water.

BEAT to smooth.

BEAT to stiff the egg whites and tartar.

POUR egg mixture over whites slowly and fold in gently.

BAKE in 9" tube pan 325 degrees 35 minutes or until done. SERVE with warm raisin sauce below.

RAISIN SAUCE: COOK together 1/2 cup

raisins in 1-1/2 cup water to tender.

DISSOLVE 3 tsp cornstarch in little cold water and add to hot mixture to thicken.

ADD 1/2 tsp vanilla and 1/2 tsp cinnamon.

EXCHANGE 1/12 of recipe = 2/3 bread -

1/3 fruit - 1/4 meat - 1-1/5 fat

APPLESAUCE CAKE

1 medium egg, beaten	2 cups flour
2 tblsp unsweet cocoa	1/2 tsp soda
1½ tsp cinnamon	1/4 tsp salt
1/2 tsp nutmeg	1/2 tsp cloves
2 tsp baking powder	1/2 cup oil
1 tsp lemon rind	1/2 cup raisins

1½ cup unsweetened applesauce
6 small walnuts, chopped
20 dates, Soak 5 minutes in hot
    water - Drain well & chop.

****

MIX oil, applesauce, egg,
together until well blended.

MIX together flour, cocoa, baking powder,
soda, salt, cinnamon, cloves & nutmeg.

ADD to flour mixture the raisins, dates,
walnuts and lemon rind.

ADD flour mixture to applesauce mixture.
MIX until well blended. (mixture will be
thick).

BAKE in greased loaf pan 325 degrees for
about 1 hour or until done.

SERVE slightly warm.

APPROXIMATE EXCHANGE - 1/24 of recipe =
1/2 bread, 1   fruit, 1 fat

**

APPLE DATE CAKE

1 cup boiling water	1½ tsp cinnamon
36 medium dates, chopped	1/2 tsp cloves
2 small apples	1 tsp soda
1/2 cup shortening	1½ cup flour,
1 egg	self-rising
1 tsp vanilla	20 small walnuts

****

SOAK dates in hot water - Add soda; Cool.

PEEL & shred apples & squeeze out juice.

CREAM shortening, egg & vanilla; Stir
in cooled dates and apples.

COMBINE dry ingredients and stir in; Add
nuts.

BAKE in greased & floured 9 X 11" pan
350 degrees about 35 minutes to done.

SPREAD WITH topping and put under broiler
just to brown.

SERVE warm

TOPPING: Combine 3 tblsp butter, 1 cup
  unsweet coconut & milk to moisten.

APPROXIMATE EXCHANGE: 1/25 th of recipe =

1/2 bread - 3/4 fruit - 1-1/2 fat

FRUIT COCKTAIL CUPCAKES

1-3/4 cup flour   2 eggs, beaten
2 tsp baking powder   1/4 cup margarine
3/4 tsp salt   1 tsp lemon extract
1/4 tsp allspice   1/2 cup coconut
1-1/2 tsp cinnamon
1 cup unsweetened fruit cocktail, drained
2/3 cup syrup from the cocktail

****

MIX flour, baking powder, salt, allspice,
and cinnamon together.

BEAT eggs and add melted margarine,
lemon extract and syrup.

ADD flour mixture and stir just until
moistened.

STIR in fruit cocktail and coconut.

FILL well greased muffin tins 2/3 full
and bake 400 degrees 20 to 25 minutes
until done.

SERVE slightly warm with little jelly
frosting from page 28.

APPROXIMATE EXCHANGE: 1/12 of recipe =

1 bread - 1/2 fruit - 1/6 meat - 1-1/3
fat not including the frosting

PINEAPPLE CARROT CUPCAKES

2 tblsp margarine, melted
3/4 cup cake flour
3/4 tsp cinnamon
1/4 tsp baking powder
12 dates, chopped
1/2 cup carrots, shredded
1/4 cup pineapple juice
1/4 cup crushed, water packed pineapple
    very well drained

1/4 tsp soda
1 egg, medium
1/8 tsp salt
1 tsp vanilla

☆☆

COMBINE margarine, egg & vanilla.

MIX dry ingredients and add margarine mixture and pineapple juice. BEAT WELL

ADD rest of ingredients and mix well.

BAKE in 8 greased muffin cups 350 degrees about 20 minutes.

SERVE SLIGHTLY WARMED

APPROXIMATE EXCHANGE - 1/8 of recipe =

3/5 bread, 1 fruit, 1/8 "B" Vegetable, 3/4 fat, 1/8 meat

SPICE CUPCAKES

1½ cups flour
1½ tsp baking powder
1½ tsp cinnamon
1/2 cup cold water
2 medium eggs
1/2 cup raisins

1/4 tsp salt
1/2 tsp nutmeg
1/4 tsp soda
1/4 tsp cloves
1/2 cup butter

****

COMBINE flour, baking powder, cinnamon, salt, nutmeg, soda, and cloves.

CUT in the butter until mixture is crumbly.

ADD water, slightly beaten eggs

MIX to blended.

ADD raisins

BAKE in greased muffin tins 350 degrees about 30 minutes or until done.

APPROXIMATE EXCHANGE - 1/12 of recipe =

3/4 bread, 2 fat, 1/6 meat, 2/3 fruit.

SERVE SLIGHTLY WARMED

WHIP TOPPING

1/2 cup skim instant dry milk
1/2 cup ice water, (See instructions in back)
1/2 tsp lemon extract
1/2 tsp vanilla
Artificial sweetener to = 3 tblsp sugar

****

IN CHILLED BOWL blend all ingredients.

WHEN moist beat at high speed until soft peaks form

APPROXIMATE EXCHANGE - Complete recipe =

1-1/2 milk exchange.

JELLY FROSTING

8 tblsp cream cheese
2 tblsp Grape jelly

BEAT cream cheese & jelly together.

APPROXIMATE EXCHANGE - 1 tblsp =

1 fat, trace of fruit

COOKIES & BARS

COCONUT COOKIES

1/2 cup shortening
1 egg, medium
2 tblsp water
1 tsp vanilla
1/2 tsp lemon extract
1/2 cup coconut

1 tsp baking powder
2 cups flour
1 tsp cinnamon
1/2 tsp salt

****

CREAM shortening; Add egg, water, vanilla and lemon extract.

MIX coconut, baking powder, flour, cinnamon and salt together.

ADD to creamed mixture and mix well.

SHAPE into rolls and chill in refrigerator.

CUT into 40 cookies and bake on ungreased cookie sheet 400 degrees about 10 minutes or to light brown.

SERVE slightly warm.

APPROXIMATE EXCHANGE:

1 cookie = 1/3 bread - 2/3 fat

CINNAMON COOKIES

5 tblsp margarine
1/4 tsp baking powder
2 tsp cinnamon
1 cup flour
2 tsp vanilla
1 tblsp water
1/4 cup raisins

****

CREAM margarine to fluffy.

MIX baking powder, cinnamon, flour
together and add to margarine. Beat.

ADD vanilla, water and raisins.

MIX well and shape dough into balls and
flatten with fork. Be sure raisins are
in dough so they do not burn.

BAKE 375 degrees on greased cookie sheet
about 12 to 15 minutes or until edges
are browned.

MAKES 30 cookies

APPROXIMATE EXCHANGE:

1 cookie = 1/5 bread - 1/2 fat - trace
of fruit

CARROT FRUIT COOKIES

1/4 cup shortening
1 egg
4 tblsp frozen orange juice concentrate
4 tblsp water
1/2 tsp orange extract
1 tsp vanilla
1 cup self-rising flour
1/4 tsp baking powder
1/4 cup dry milk powder, non-fat
1 tsp cinnamon
1 small banana, chopped very fine
12 dates, chopped fine
1 cup shredded carrots
18 small walnuts, chopped fine

****

CREAM shortening; Add egg, orange juice,
water & flavorings.

MIX flour, baking powder, milk powder,
& cinnamon.

ADD to creamed mixture the banana,
dates, carrots & nuts.

ADD dry ingredients and mix well.

DROP on greased cookie sheet & bake
375 degrees 12 minutes.

SERVE warm

EXCHANGE: 1/4 of recipe or 9 cookies =

1/4 bread - 1/4 meat - 1/5 milk -
2-1/2 fruit - 1/2 B Veg - 4 fat

MAKES 36 cookies

OATMEAL COOKIES

1-1/2 cups flour
1-1/2 tsp cinnamon
1/2 tsp salt
2 tsp baking powder
2/3 cup shortening, melted & cooled
2 eggs, beaten, room temperature
1-1/2 cups quick oatmeal, uncooked
1/2 cup water
1 tsp vanilla
1/4 cup dry milk powder
1/2 cup currants, soaked & drained
18 small walnuts, chopped

****

MIX flour, cinnamon, salt, baking powder,
and dry milk powder.

MIX melted shortening, eggs, and oatmeal
and mix well; Add water & vanilla.

ADD 1/2 flour mixture; then currants,
and nuts; Then add rest of flour.

DROP on greased baking sheet and bake
400 degrees about 10 to 12 minutes.

SERVE warm

EXCHANGE: 1/4 recipe or 9 cookies =

3-3/4 bread - 1 fruit - 1/5 milk - 1/4
meat - 8-1/2 fat

MAKES 36 cookies

PUMPKIN COOKIES

1 cup shortening
1 cup pumpkin, canned
1 egg
1 tsp vanilla
2 cups flour
1/4 tsp allspice
1/2 tsp salt
1/2 tsp nutmeg
1/2 tsp soda
1 tsp baking powder
1 tsp cinnamon
1 cup currants
18 small nuts, chopped

****

SOAK currants in hot water 5 minutes, Drain.

CREAM shortening; Add pumpkin, egg and
vanilla and beat together.

MIX flour, allspice, salt, nutmeg, soda,
baking powder and cinnamon.

ADD to creamed mixture and mix well.

ADD currants and nuts.

MAKES 48 cookies

BEST served slightly warm

APPROXIMATE EXCHANGE: 1 cookie =

1/3 bread - 1/6 fruit - trace "B" Veg -
1 fat

APPLESAUCE BRAN COOKIES

1-3/4 cup cake flour   1 tsp soda
1/2 tsp salt   1/2 cup margarine
1 tsp cinnamon   1 egg
1/2 tsp nutmeg   1 cup All-Bran
1/2 tsp cloves   1/2 cup raisins
1 cup unsweetened applesauce

****

SIFT together the flour, salt, cinnamon, nutmeg, cloves and soda.

MIX margarine and egg until light and fluffy.

THEN add flour mixture and applesauce alternately, mixing well after each addition.

FOLD in raisins and all-bran.

DROP onto greased cookie sheet about 1 inch apart.

BAKE 375 degrees about 20 minutes or until golden brown.

COOL on racks. SERVE slightly warmed

APPROXIMATE EXCHANGE: 1/36 of recipe =

1/3 bread - 1/6 fruit - 2/3 fat

SWEET POTATO COOKIES

1 cup shortening
1 cup Sweet potatoes, cooked & mashed
1 egg
1 tsp vanilla
2 cup flour
1/4 tsp allspice
1/2 tsp salt
1/2 tsp nutmeg
1/2 tsp soda
1 tsp baking powder
1 tsp cinnamon
1 cup raisins
18 small walnuts, chopped

****

SOAK raisins in hot water 5 minutes, Drain.

CREAM shortening; Add sweet potatoes,
egg and vanilla; Beat.

MIX flour, allspice, salt, nutmeg, soda,
baking powder and cinnamon.

ADD to creamed mixture and mix well.

ADD raisins and nuts.

MAKES 48 cookies

BEST served slightly warm.

APPROXIMATE EXCHANGE: 1 cookie -

1/3 bread - 1/6 fruit - 1/10 "B" or #2
Vegetable - 1 fat

RAISIN ORANGE COOKIES

1/4 cup margarine   2 cups flour
2 tsp baking powder   1/2 tsp salt
2 tsp cinnamon   1 egg, medium
1/2 cup orange juice
3/4 tsp grated orange rind
3/4 cup raisins, chopped
6 small walnuts, chopped

****

CREAM margarine and egg together.

MIX together flour, baking powder, salt,
cinnamon, & orange rind.

COMBINE flour & egg mixture alternately
with orange juice.

ADD rest of ingredients.

DROP on greased sheet & flatten with fork.

PUSH RAISINS INTO DOUGH so they don't burn.

BAKE 375 degrees about 20 minutes.

EAT SLIGHTLY WARM

APPROXIMATE EXCHANGE - 1/36 of recipe =
1/3 bread, 1/5 fruit, 1/3 fat

DATE COOKIES

2 tblsp margarine, melted   1 cup flour
1 medium egg, beaten   1/4 tsp salt
1 tsp baking powder   1/4 cup water
1 tsp cinnamon   8 dates
1/2 tsp vanilla   chopped
12 small walnuts, chopped

****

MIX together dates, nuts, margarine, egg, water & vanilla.

MIX flour, baking powder, salt & cinnamon.

ADD flour mixture to first mixture. MIX.

BAKE on greased sheets 350 degrees 15 to 20 minutes.

SERVE slightly warm
MAKES 18 cookies

APPROXIMATE EXCHANGE -   1/18 of recipe =

1/3 bread, 1/5 fruit, 1/2 fat, trace meat

**

OATMEAL & APPLESAUCE COOKIES

1/2 cup unsweet applesauce
1/4 cup cooking oil
1/2 cup quick oatmeal
1-1/2 tsp cinnamon
1/4 tsp nutmeg
1 tsp allspice
1/2 cup raisins

1/2 cup flour
1/2 tsp soda
1/4 tsp salt
1 egg, medium
1 tsp cloves
1 tsp vanilla

****

MIX flour, cinnamon, soda, salt, nutmeg, cloves, allspice, oatmeal & raisins.

ADD applesauce, oil, egg, vanilla

MIX just to moisten.

DROP on greased sheets.

BAKE 375 degrees about 12 minutes.

MAKES 24 cookies

APPROXIMATE EXCHANGE - 1/24 of recipe =

1/5 bread, 1/5 fruit, 1/2 fat, trace meat

Best served slightly **warm**

RAISIN DROP COOKIES

1/4 cup whole wheat flour
1/4 cup white flour
1/2 tsp baking powder
1/2 cup margarine
1 cup quick oatmeal
1/2 tsp cinnamon

2 eggs
1/2 tsp salt
1 tsp vanilla
12 small
   walnuts
     chopped

3/4 cup raisins, Soak in hot water
   5 minutes - Drain well & chop.

****

MELT margarine. Beat in eggs & vanilla.

SIFT TOGETHER flours, baking powder, salt, and cinnamon.

MIX into the dry ingredients the raisins, walnuts & oatmeal.

ADD dry ingredients to egg mixture and blend well.

DROP on greased sheets & bake 350 degrees about 12 to 15 minutes.

MAKES 48 cookies

APPROXIMATE EXCHANGE - 1 cookie =

1/7 bread, 1/8 fruit, 1/2 fat, trace meat

SERVE slightly warm

**

KRISPIE DATE BARS

1 cup dates (about 36)
1/4 cup butter or margarine
2 cups Rice Krispies
1 tsp vanilla
1 egg
18 small walnuts, chopped

****

SOAK dates in hot water 5 minutes; Drain
and snip with scissors into saucepan.

ADD margarine and simmer about 3 minutes
stirring constantly.

BEAT egg in bowl; Then beat in hot date
mixture and stir well.

ADD vanilla; COOL to room temperature.

ADD Rice Krispies and nuts.

SPREAD in buttered pan and chill.

CUT into bars.

EXCHANGE:

1/24 = Trace bread - 3/4 fruit - 2/3 fat

FIG BARS

1-1/2 cup flour   3/4 cup butter
1-1/2 cup oatmeal   18 small walnuts
1/2 tsp cinnamon   1/8 tsp salt

****

MIX flour, oats, cinnamon & salt; ADD
chopped nuts and butter and mix until
crumbly.

PACK 1/2 mixture in greased 9 X 9" pan.

SPREAD filling over and top with rest
of crumbly mixture; Pack down.

BAKE 375 degrees about 25 minutes to
light brown.

CUT into 36 pieces.

FILLING:

COOK 1-1/4 cup (about 40) figs in 1-3/4
     cup boiling water until tender;
     Mash and cook until slightly thick.

     ADD 2/3 tsp lemon extract, 2/3 tsp
     cinnamon, 1/4 tsp salt & 18 small
     chopped walnuts.

EXCHANGE:

1 piece = 1/2 bread - 1-1/10 fruit -
1-1/6 fat

PIES

PUMPKIN PIE

1-1/2 cups canned pumpkin   2 eggs
1-3/4 cups evaporated milk   ½ tsp cloves
1/2 tsp allspice
1   tsp cinnamon
1/2 tsp ginger
1/2 tsp nutmeg

Sweetener to = 3/4 cup sugar (see below)

****

COMBINE pumpkin, eggs, milk, cloves, ginger
nutmeg, allspice, cinnamon and sweetener.

BEAT to smooth.

POUR into chilled unbaked 9" pie crust.

BAKE 425 degrees 15 minutes.

REDUCE heat to 350 degrees and bake 35
minutes more or until knife inserted in
center comes out clean.

MAKES 8 servings

APPROXIMATE EXCHANGE - 1/8 with crust =

1-1/4 bread, 1/2 milk, 1/4 meat, 3¼ fat

TO CONVERT TO USE WITHOUT SWEETENER

OMIT sweetener and add 1/2 cup coconut
and 20 fine chopped dates.

ADD: 1/5 bread - 1/12 fruit & 1/3 fat to
     the exchanges.

CRUSTLESS APPLESAUCE PIE

2 eggs, well beaten
1/2 cup applesauce
1/3 cup skim milk
1 tblsp butter
1/4 tsp salt
1 tsp vanilla
1 tsp cinnamon
1/2 cup raisins, chopped
18 small walnuts, chopped
1-1/4 cups Bran flakes

****

MIX eggs, applesauce, milk, butter,
salt, vanilla, and cinnamon together.

ADD raisins and nuts.

FOLD in bran flakes

POUR into slightly buttered 8" pyrex
pie pan.

BAKE 375 degrees about 25 minutes or
until top is set.

SERVE with whip cream or Ice cream.

EXCHANGE:

1/5 of recipe = 1/2 bread - 1 fruit -
Trace milk - 1/2 meat - 1-1/2 fat -

(Exchange does not include topping)

APPLE RAISIN PIE

8 small apples
1 tsp cinnamon
1/3 cup raisins
2 tblsp breadcrumbs

****

PEEL and shred the apples.

SQUEEZE all juice out of the apples.

ADD raisins.

PLACE in 8" unbaked pastry lined pie pan.

SPRINKLE with crumbs and cinnamon &
with a fork work into apples slightly.

COVER with foil and prick holes in top.

BAKE 375 degrees about 30 minutes or
until apples are done.

EXCHANGE: 1/8 of pie without crust =

1-1/3 fruit - Trace bread

(For exchange on crust follow those
 listed on recipe you use)

SOUR CREAM RAISIN PIE

1 unbaked 8" pie shell (optional)
2 eggs
1 cup dairy sour cream
1 tsp vanilla
1/4 tsp cinnamon & 1/4 tsp nutmeg
1/4 tsp salt
1 cup raisins
20 small walnuts, chopped

****

BEAT eggs, sour cream, vanilla, salt, cinnamon and nutmeg together until well blended.

STIR in raisins and nuts.

POUR into pie shell and place on rack below oven center.

BAKE 375 degrees about 40 minutes or just until set.

COOL

EXCHANGE: Complete recipe - 8 fruit - 1 meat - 12-1/3 fat   PLUS: Pastry

(Can be baked without pastry and served as a pudding if desired)

STRAWBERRY PIE

3/4 cup unsweet strawberries, fresh sliced
1 pkg artificial sweetened strawberry jello
Granulated sweetener to = 1/4 cup sugar
1 cup evaporated skim milk
dash of salt

****

DISSOLVE jello in 1½ cups boiling water.

STIR in salt & sweetener. CHILL over ice
water until syrupy.

POUR evaporated milk in a loaf pan & put
in freezer until crystals form at edges.

BEAT milk in chilled bowl until stiff.

FOLD in jello until no streaks remain.

FOLD in Strawberries carefully.

TURN into baked 9" shell & CHILL 3 hours.

APPROXIMATE EXCHANGE - 1/8 of recipe =

1 bread, 1/4 milk, 1/8 fruit, 2¼ fat

NOTE: If Graham cracker crust is used.
EXCHANGE would be 3/4 bread, 3/4 fat,
1/8 fruit & 1/4 milk.

FRUIT COCKTAIL PIE

1/4 cup cornstarch   1/2 tsp vanilla
1/4 tsp salt   2 tblsp margarine
2 cups 2% milk   1 tsp cinnamon
3 egg yolks
1 cup coconut
1 cup drained unsweetened fruit cocktail

****

COMBINE in saucepan, cornstarch and salt.

SCALD milk and add slowly to saucepan;
Cook slow to thick about 3 minutes.

ADD a little to slightly beaten egg yolks
and then pour into mixture & cook 1 minute.

REMOVE from heat and add margarine and
stir to melted. ADD 2/3 cup coconut.

ADD vanilla, cinnamon and fruit cocktail.

COOL slightly and pour into prepared
graham cracker crust and sprinkle top
with rest of coconut.

SERVE chilled

APPROXIMATE EXCHANGE: 1/8 of pie plus
crust = 1/2 bread - 1/4 fruit - 1/4 milk -
1-3/4 meat - 2 fat (Not including crust)

PINEAPPLE CREAM PIE

2 cups skim milk, scalded	3 egg yolks
1/4 cup cornstarch	1/4 tsp salt
1/2 tsp vanilla	

1 cup pineapple, crushed, very well drained.
 (packed in its own juice)
Artificial sweetener to = 3½ tblsp sugar
****

COMBINE in saucepan, cornstarch, salt &
stirring slowly add hot milk & cook slow
until thick... ADD sweetener

BEAT slightly the yolks & add little of
hot mixture stirring in and then add to
the mixture and continue cooking 1 minute.

REMOVE from heat & add vanilla & fruit.

COOL slightly and pour into 9" graham crust.

CHILL

APPROXIMATE EXCHANGE - 1/8 of pie=

1 bread, 1/4 fruit, 1/4 milk, 1/6 meat,
1 fat

TO CONVERT TO USE WITHOUT SWEETENER

Omit sweetener and add 1 cup coconut after
removing from heat.

ADD: 1/3 bread and 3/4 fat to exchanges

APPLE PIE

6 small apples	2 tblsp flour
1/8 tsp nutmeg	1 tsp cinnamon
dash salt	1 - 9" unbaked pastry

Brown sugar substitute to = 1/2 to 3/4 cup sugar

****

PEEL and slice apples. ADD nutmeg, flour, salt and cinnamon.

PLACE into unbaked pastry.

COVER with aluminum foil. Poke holes in top for steam to escape.

BAKE 350 degrees about 50 minutes or until apples are tender.

APPROXIMATE EXCHANGE - 1/8 of pie =

1-1/9 bread, 3/4 fruit, 2¼ fat

TO CONVERT TO USE WITHOUT SWEETENER

Omit sweetener and add 3/4 cup raisins to the apples.

ADD 3/4 fruit to exchanges

PIE CRUST

1-1/4 cup flour   1-1/4 tsp salt
6 tblsp margarine   5 tblsp water

****

COMBINE flour & salt. CUT in margarine until crumbly.

ADD water slowly until dough is moistened & holds together.

ROLL on floured pastry board.

MAKES 1 - 9" pie shell

APPROXIMATE EXCHANGE - 1/8 of shell = 1 bread, 2¼ fat.

GRAHAM CRACKER CRUST

2 tblsp margarine   2 tblsp warm water
Granulated sweetener to = 3 tblsp sugar
1 cup Graham cracker crumbs

****

MELT margarine: Remove from heat & add water & sweetener.

STIR in crumbs until thoroughly combined.

PRESS in bottom & sides of 9" pie pan.

BAKE 400 degrees 6 minutes. COOL

APPROXIMATE EXCHANGE - 1/8 of recipe =

2/3 bread , 3/4 fat

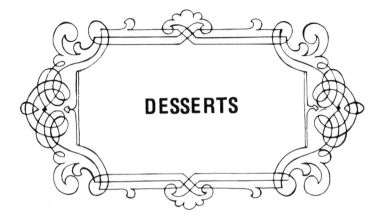

DESSERTS

BLUEBERRY BREAD PUDDING

4 cups blueberries, fresh or frozen
1/4 cup flour
4 cups hot skim milk
4 slices coarse bread,
dash salt
2 tblsp margarine
1-1/2 tsp cinnamon
3/4 cup coconut

****

WASH & drain berries and spread out on plate.

SPRINKLE with flour and let set 1/2 hour .

POUR milk over bread cubes.

ADD salt, cinnamon and berries
and add coconut and mix well.

POUR into greased 2-1/2 quart baking dish
and dot with butter.

BAKE 350 degrees about 45 minutes.

SERVE warm with little cream or Ice
cream from your allowance.

EXCHANGE: 1/12 recipe = 2/3 bread - 1/3
milk - 2/3 fruit - 9/10 fat (not including
any cream or Ice cream used)

PRUNE APPLESAUCE BREAD PUDDING

4 tblsp margarine
2 cups unsweetened applesauce
2 eggs
2 slices diced, whole wheat bread
2 tsp cinnamon
1/8 tsp nutmeg
12 prunes
2 tblsp prune juice

****

MELT margarine to sizzling...

ADD bread and saute until brown and
slightly crisp.

BEAT eggs, add applesauce, cinnamon,
nutmeg.

COOK prunes in 1/2 cup water until
tender.

CHOP fine and add to mixture. Add
prune juice from cooking prunes.

FOLD in the bread and pour into
greased casserole dish.

BAKE 350 degrees about 35 minutes
uncovered until lightly brown on top.

SERVE slightly warm with little cream.
        or Ice cream from allowance

EXCHANGE: 1/12 of recipe = 1/6 bread

3/4 fruit - 1/6 meat - 1-1/6 fat not
including any cream for topping.

APPLE BREAD PUDDING

1 cup milk, skimmed
1 slice bread crust
1½ tsp cinnamon
1 small apple,
  peeled & chopped

1/2 tsp vanilla
1 egg, medium
2 tblsp raisins

****

SCALD milk & cool slightly.

ADD slightly beaten egg & vanilla.

BREAK bread into baking dish & add raisins,
cinnamon & apple.

POUR milk mixture over bread.

PLACE in baking dish and put dish in
a pan of water.

BAKE 350 degrees 45 to 60 minutes to done.
Apples should be tender & custard set.

SERVE slightly warmed with little Ice
cream from your allowance.

APPROXIMATE EXCHANGE - 1/4 of recipe =

1/4 bread, 1/4 milk, 1/2 fruit, 1/4 meat
1/8 fat

PINEAPPLE BREAD PUDDING

3 slices French bread
1 cup skim milk
1 egg, separated
2 tblsp margarine
1 tsp vanilla

1/2 cup raisins
1/2 tsp cinnamon
1/4 tsp cloves
dash nutmeg
1/8 tsp salt

1/2 cup coconut, unsweetened
1 cup crushed and drained Pineapple

****

COOK and stir for 2 minutes: The bread
crumbled and milk in saucepan; Cool
slightly.

BEAT IN: egg yolk, margarine, vanilla,
cinnamon, cloves and nutmeg.

ADD Pineapple, raisins and coconut.

WHIP until stiff egg white and salt.

FOLD in lightly.

PLACE in greased dish and bake 375 degrees
about 35 to 45 minutes.

SERVE warm with little cream if desired.

EXCHANGE: Complete recipe = 4½ bread, 1
medium fat meat, 1 milk, 6 fruit, 9 fat

APPLE RAISIN PUDDING

2 slices coarse bread cubes (About 2 cups)
1 cup skim milk
2 small apples chopped (About 1-1/2 cups)
3/4 cup raisins
1/4 cup flour
1/4 tsp each: Cloves and nutmeg
1/2 tsp cinnamon
1 tsp Brandy extract
3 eggs, slightly beaten

****

MIX bread with milk and raisins and heat
until milk is absorbed.

ADD apples,

MIX together flour, cloves, nutmeg ,cinnamon.
stir into mixture.

ADD eggs and extract.

POUR into heavy buttered baking dish and
bake 375 degrees about 45 minutes.

SERVE warm with little cream.

EXCHANGE: COMPLETE RECIPE = 4-1/2 bread
8 fruit - 1 milk - 3 meat - 1-1/2 fat.

(To determine exchange for each serving
divide by number of servings you want)

(Cream for topping not included in
exchanges listed)

APPLE OATMEAL PUDDING

6 small cooking apples
1 tsp cinnamon
1/2 tsp nutmeg
1/2 tsp salt
1/3 cup water
1/2 tsp soda
1 cup quick-cooking oatmeal
1/3 cup margarine
1/2 cup raisins

****

PEEL, core and slice thin the apples -
Mix with raisins and place in 6 X 10"
baking dish.

COMBINE cinnamon, nutmeg & 1/4 tsp salt
and sprinkle over apple mixture.

POUR water over apples.

COMBINE oatmeal, soda & 1/4 tsp salt;
work in margarine to make a crumbly
mixture.

SPREAD over apples and work in slightly
with a fork.

BAKE 375 degrees for 40 minutes.

SERVE WARM

EXCHANGE: Complete recipe = 3½ bread -
10 fruit - 15 fat

(Divide by desired number of servings)

PEACH RICE PUDDING

2½ tblsp uncooked rice
1 cup whole milk
1/2 medium peach, canned in water

1 tsp vanilla
1/4 tsp cinnamon

****

WASH rice in cool water and place in small casserole.

POUR 1/2 cup milk over & set casserole in a pan of water.

BAKE 350 degrees until crust forms.

STIR and add 1/4 cup milk and continue baking again until crust forms.

STIR and add 1/4 cup milk, peach, vanilla & cinnamon.

CONTINUE baking until rice is tender, Stir if needed. (If rice gets to dry add a little more milk)

SERVE slightly warm

APPROXIMATE EXCHANGE - 1/2 of recipe =

1/2 bread, 1/2 milk, 1/4 fruit, 1 fat

APPLE PEANUT CRUNCH

4 small sweet apples	2 tblsp flour
1/4 cup raisins	1/8 tsp salt
1-1/2 tblsp water	2 tblsp margarine
1/3 cup oatmeal	20 small peanuts
2 tblsp crunchy peanut butter	

****

PEEL and slice apples and place in 9 X 9"
buttered baking dish, Add raisins and
sprinkle with water.

BAKE 375 degrees for about 15 minutes.

MIX oatmeal, flour, salt,peanut butter,
margarine and chopped peanuts to make
a crumbly mixture.

SPRINKLE over top of apples and with
fork stir in just slightly.

RETURN to oven and continue baking
until apples are done about 30 minutes.

SERVE warm with Ice cream or cream.

EXCHANGE COMPLETE RECIPE:

1-1/3 bread - 6 fruit - 1 meat - 9 fat

To determine amount of exchange in each
serving divide by desired number of
servings.

(Topping not included in exchange listing)

PEACH CRUNCH

4 cups canned sliced unsweet peaches
1 cup corn flakes
3/4 cup unsweetened coconut
3/4 tsp cinnamon
2 tblsp margarine

****

DRAIN peaches and place in shallow 6
cup baking dish.

CRUSH cornflakes and mix with coconut
and cinnamon.

SPRINKLE over peaches.

DOT with margarine.

WITH fork work in the crumb mixture
into the peaches just slightly.

BAKE 350 degrees about 25 minutes or
until bubbly hot.

SERVE warm with cream or Ice cream.

EXCHANGE: Complete recipe =

8 fruit, 3½ bread,
10½ fat

MAKES about 10 servings

APPLE DESSERT

1 small apple	1 tblsp raisins
2 graham crackers	cinnamon

****

CHOP peeled apple into baking dish & sprinkle with cinnamon.

COVER with foil.

BAKE 350 degrees 30 minutes.

ADD raisins.

CRUSH crackers and spread over top of apples working into apples a little.

SPRINKLE with cinnamon.

CONTINUE baking uncovered about 15 minutes or until apples are tender.

IF crackers are getting too brown - cover lightly with foil.

SERVE slightly warm with little Ice cream from your allowance.

APPROXIMATE EXCHANGE - 1/2 of recipe =

3/4 fruit, 1/2 bread Plus Ice cream

DATE APPLESAUCE DESSERT

TOAST 4 slices bread in oven - Put in blender and reduce to crumbs.

ADD: 1/4 tsp cinnamon, 1/8 tsp nutmeg
2 tblsp margarine, melted.

MIX together and put 1/2 in bottom of buttered casserole dish.

SOAK 10 dates in hot water - Drain and cut up.

MIX with 1 cup unsweetened applesauce, 1/2 tsp cinnamon & 1 tblsp chopped walnuts.

SPREAD over crumbs, then top with the rest of the crumbs.

BAKE 350 degrees about 30 minutes.

SERVE hot or cold

EXCHANGE ON COMPLETE RECIPE:

4 bread - 7 fruit - 7 fat

APPLE CRISP

5 small apples   2-1/2 tblsp flour
1/2 tsp cinnamon   2 tblsp margarine
1/2 cup quick oatmeal
Brown sugar substitute to = 2 tblsp
                            brown sugar
Granulated sweetener to = 1/3 cup sugar

****

IN CASSEROLE mix thinly sliced peeled
apples and brown sugar substitute.

IN BOWL mix oatmeal, flour, cinnamon,
granulated sweetener & margarine.

MIX until crumble and sprinkle over
apples.

BAKE 350 degrees about 45 minutes or
until apples are tender. SERVE WARM.

APPROXIMATE EXCHANGE - 1/8 recipe =

1/3 bread, 2/3 fruit, 3/4 fat

TO CONVERT TO USE WITHOUT SWEETENER

OMIT sweeteners and add 2/3 cup raisins
to the apples.

ADD 3/4 fruit to the exchanges

PEACH DESSERT

3/4 cup drained, water packed peaches
2 graham crachers, crushed
1½ tsp margarine, melted
3 small walnuts, chopped
cinnamon

****

CHOP peaches and place in small pyrex pan.
Sprinkle with cinnamon.

MIX together crackers, margarine, & nuts.

SPREAD over peaches & sprinkle with
cinnamon.

BAKE 350 degrees about 20 minutes.

SERVE slightly warm with a little Ice
cream from your allowance.

APPROXIMATE EXCHANGE - 1/2 of recipe =
1/2 bread, 3/4 fruit, 1 fat

BANANA CUSTARD

1/2 cup whole milk   1/4 tsp vanilla
1 medium egg, slightly beaten
1/4 tsp cinnamon
1/2 small banana, sliced

****

SCALD milk.   Cool slightly.

ADD egg, cinnamon, vanilla & banana.

RINSE custard cups with cold water &
pour mixture in them.

SET cups in pan of water & bake 350
degrees until knife inserted in center
comes out clean.

MAKES 2 servings.

APPROXIMATE EXCHANGE - 1/2 of recipe =

1/4 milk, 1/2 fruit, 1/2 meat, 3/4 fat

PEACH COBBLER

3 cups dietetic canned
  peaches

1 tsp lemon juice
1/4 cup shortening
1/4 cup skim milk

2 tsp baking powder

Artificial sweetener to = 1 tsp sugar

1/8 tsp nutmeg
1/4 tsp cinnamon
1 cup cake flour
1 egg , medium
2 tsp margarine
          melted

****

COMBINE drained sliced peaches, juice,
nutmeg & margarine. SPREAD in 8" pan.

MIX flour, baking powder and work in the
shortening until crumbly.

STIR in beaten egg, milk & sweetener.

SPREAD over peaches and sprinkle with
cinnamon.

BAKE 375 degrees about 40 minutes.

MAKES 12 servings

APPROXIMATE EXCHANGE - 1/12 of recipe =

1/2 bread, 1/2 fruit, 1-1/6 fat, 1/12 meat
trace of milk

SERVE SLIGHTLY WARM WITH a little Ice
cream from your daily allowance

  **

RHUBARB PUDDING

3 cups rhubarb, diced   3 tblsp water
2 tsp baking powder   1 egg
1/2 cup skim milk   1 cup flour
2 tblsp shortening   1/2 tsp salt

Artificial sweetener to = 1-1/2 cup sugar

****

MIX rhubarb, sweetener to = 1 cup sugar,
and water.

PLACE in greased casserole and put in
oven at 350 degrees while mixing rest.

CREAM shortening, sweetener to = 1/2 cup
sugar. ADD egg.

MIX flour, baking powder, & salt.

ADD alternately into creamed mixture
with the milk.

POUR over rhubarb and continue baking
about 40 minutes.

MAKES 12 servings

SERVE slightly warm with a little Ice
cream from your daily allowance.

APPROXIMATE EXCHANGE - 1/12 of recipe =

1/2 bread, 1/12 meat, trace milk, 1/2
vegetable from list #2, 1/2 fat

WAFFLES

1 tblsp margarine, melted   3/4 cup flour
1 tsp baking powder   1/4 tsp salt
2/3 cup skim milk   1 egg, medium

Granulated artificial sweetener to = 2 tbsp sugar.

****

MIX dry ingredients together.

IN SEPARATE BOWL beat eggs, milk & margarine.

STIR mixtures together until batter is almost smooth.

MAKES 5 WAFFLES

APPROXIMATE EXCHANGE - 1/5 of recipe =

1 bread, 1/5 meat, 1/7 milk, 3/4 fat

MAPLE SYRUP

COMBINE 1-1/2 cups cold water, 1 tblsp cornstarch, 1/8 tsp salt, 1 tsp maple flavoring.

BRING TO BOIL. REMOVE from heat and add liquid sweetener to = 2/3 cup sugar.

APPROXIMATE EXCHANGE - complete recipe =

1/2 bread.

FROZEN BANANAS

Bananas
1 pkg chocolate chips
1/2 tsp parafin

Choose firm, ripe bananas

PEEL and cut into 3 pieces - Put popsicle stick in each.

MELT chocolate chips and parafin.

DIP bananas in chocolate and then in some chopped nuts.

PLACE standing on plate and freeze solid.

STORE in plastic bags. SERVE FROZEN.

VARIETY:

COAT bananas with orange juice concentrate.

PLACE in freezer to chill 15 minutes.

ROLL in chopped nuts.

SET in freezer to firm.

SERVE FROZEN.

EXCHANGE: Depends on number of bananas and other ingredients used.

ORANGE MILKSHAKE

1/3 cup frozen orange juice concentrate
1/3 cup powdered milk (nonfat)
3/4 cup ice water
1/2 cup crushed ice
1 tblsp creamy peanut butter

****

COMBINE orange juice, powdered milk,
ice water, ice and peanut butter in
container of blender.

TURN on high and process until good
and frothy.

EXCHANGE: Complete recipe = 1 milk -
2½ fruit - 1/2 meat - 1 fat

VARIETY:

USE Grape juice concentrate in place
of Orange juice.

ADD 1 ripe peeled banana before blending.

ADD little Ice cream from your allowance
after blended.

BLUEBERRY YOGURT FLOAT

1/4 cup yogurt, 2% plain
1/4 cup skim milk
1/2 cup Blueberries, fresh or frozen
1/8 tsp almond extract
1 ice cube, crushed

****

IN blender container place yogurt, milk, blueberries and extract.

COVER and blend at high speed until mixture is frothy.

ADD ice and blend to smooth.

SERVE immediately

EXCHANGE:

1/2 milk - 1 fruit - 1/4 fat

IF DESIRED: Add couple teaspoons of Ice cream from your allowance.

VARIATION

SUBSTITUTE strawberries, peaches or raspberries in place of blueberries.

Be sure to adjust your exchanges if any variations made.

BANANA MILKSHAKE

1/3 cup nonfat dry milk (undiluted)
1/3 cup ice water
1 ripe small banana
1/4 tsp vanilla
4 ice cubes

****

MEASURE milk powder and ice water into container of electric blender.

COVER and process at low speed until well mixed.

PEEL banana and cut up into small pieces and add to milk.

COVER and blend to smooth.

CRUSH ice cubes and add to mixture, then turn on high speed and process until frothy.

EXCHANGE: Complete recipe = 1 milk - 2 fruit.

(If desired add a little Ice cream from your diet allowance)

STRAWBERRY MILKSHAKE

1 cup frozen strawberries, unsweetened
1/2 cup skim milk
1/4 tsp vanilla
Liquid artificial sweetener to taste

****

MIX 1/2 strawberries with milk in blender.

ADD rest of strawberries, vanilla, sweetener.

BLEND until berries are crushed and mixture
is consistency of milkshake.

APPROXIMATE EXCHANGE - complete recipe =

1-1/4 fruit, 1/2 milk

SODA POP MILKSHAKE

1/3 cup powdered skim milk
3/4 cup cold or Ice water
1/2 can sugarfree soda pop - Any flavor

PUT in blender until powder dissolves. ADD
some ice chips & blend to thick.

COMPLETE RECIPE = 1 milk exchange

STRAWBERRY SHERBET

1 (12 oz) can sugarfree Strawberry soda
1-1/2 cups unsweetened Strawberries
1/2 cup dry powdered skim milk
Artificial sweetener to = 6 tsp sugar

****

BEAT together the soda, strawberries, dry milk and sweetener.

PUT in freezing container and place in freezer.

BEAT about 4 times during freezing.

ALLOW to freeze just to medium hard stage.

IF it gets to hard, let set out 15 minutes before serving.

MAKES 6 servings

APPROXIMATE EXCHANGE - 1/6 of recipe =

1/4 milk - 1/3 fruit

VANILLA ICE CREAM

| 1 cup whole milk | 2 eggs |
| 2 cups light cream | 2 tsp vanilla |

Just under 1/8 tsp salt or to taste

Artificial sweetener to taste

****

SCALD milk in a double boiler.

BEAT eggs & add salt.

POUR slowly into hot milk stirring constantly.

COOK until mixture coats a spoon. COOL.

ADD cream, vanilla and sweetener.

PLACE in freezer tray and beat at least 4 times during freezing time.

MAKES 12 servings

APPROXIMATE EXCHANGES -1/12 of recipe =

1/12 milk, 1/6 meat, 1-1/2 fat

**

CHOCOLATE ICE CREAM

1 tblsp cornstarch	1/2 cup water
3/4 cup Evp whole milk	dash salt
1 cup heavy cream	1/2 tsp vanilla
1 square unsweetened chocolate	

Artificial sweetener to = 1/2 cup sugar

****

DISSOLVE cornstarch in water. ADD sweetener & salt and cook until mixture boils & gets thick. Stir constantly.

COOL & refrigerate.

WHIP chilled evaporated milk until it gets thick.

ADD cornstarch mixture and vanilla.

MELT the chocolate and cool.

WHIP the heavy cream.

FOLD creams & chocolate together enough to blend.

POUR into freezing containers & freeze 3 to 4 hours.

APPROXIMATE EXCHANGE - 1/8 of recipe =

1/16 bread, 1/6 milk, 2-1/2 fat

**

CONFECTIONS, JAMS

FIG BALLS

20 dried figs
1/4 cup raisins
10 small walnuts
4 tblsp unsweetened coconut

****

GRIND figs, raisins & nuts together &
mix with little orange juice to moist
and sticks together well.

ROLL in coconut

1/12 recipe = Trace bread - 1-3/4 fruit
1/4 fat

****

DATE SNACKS

24 dates, pitted
6 small walnuts
4 tblsp coconut

CHOP dates. Roll in coconut - Press
1/4 of walnut into each.

1/12 recipe = Trace bread - 1 fruit -
                1/5 fat

PEANUT BUTTER CANDY

2 tblsp chunky peanut butter
1 graham cracker
2 tblsp skim milk
1 tsp vanilla
4 tblsp raisins, chopped
2 tblsp coconut, unsweetened

****

CREAM peanut butter and 1 tblsp milk
until smooth.

ADD vanilla and raisins.

CRUMBLE cracker and work in then add
enough milk to make it stick together
well.

FORM into balls and roll in coconut.

CHILL in refrigerator

APPROXIMATE EXCHANGE: Complete recipe =

9/10 bread - 1/8 milk - 1 meat -
2 fruit - 2-1/2 fat

FRUIT CONFECTIONS

12 prunes, pitted   18 figs
12 tblsp raisins   1/4 tsp salt
18 small walnuts, chopped fine
2 tblsp cold coffee

****

GRIND together the prunes, figs & raisins.

ADD walnuts, salt & coffee.

KNEAD with fingers.

DAMPEN hands and form into 18 balls.

Approximate EXCHANGE - 1 ball =

1-2/3 fruit, 1/6 fat

APPLE BUTTER

3/4 cup hot water   1 tsp cinnamon
1/2 tblsp lemon juice   1/4 tsp cloves
                           1/8 tsp allspice

8 small apples (about 6 cups)
Artificial sweetener to = 3/4 cup sugar **or**
to taste

****

IN SAUCEPAN combine peeled, sliced cooking
apples and the water.

SIMMER 15 to 20 minutes until tender.

MASH the apples and juice.

ADD lemon juice, cinnamon, cloves,
allspice and sweetner.

COOK slowly until thick. About 45 minutes .

Stir frequently.

APPROXIMATE EXCHANGE - 1 tsp = trace fruit

GRAPE JELLY

1 envelope unflavored gelatin

1-1/2 cups unsweetened grape juice

1/2 cup water

1 cinnamon stick

2 whole cloves

Artificial sweetener to = 1/3 cup sugar or to taste

****

IN PAN soften gelatin in grape juice and water.

ADD cinnamon and cloves.

STIR to dissolve gelatin and cook at a rolling boil about 1 minute.

REMOVE from heat and add sweetener.

REMOVE cinnamon and cloves.

STORE in refrigerator.

APPROXIMATE EXCHANGE - 1 tblsp of jelly =

1/5 fruit

APPLE JELLY

4 tsp unflavored gelatin

2 cups unsweetened apple juice

1-1/2 tsp lemon juice

few drops yellow food coloring

Artificial sweetener to = 3/4 cup sugar or
to taste

****

SOFTEN gelatin in 1/2 cup of cool juice.

BRING rest of juice to a boil.

REMOVE FROM burner and add **gelatin** and
stir to dissolve.

ADD lemon juice, sweetener and coloring.

STORE IN REFRIGERATOR

APPROXIMATE EXCHANGE - 4 tblsp =

3/4 fruit

STRAWBERRY JAM

2 envelopes unflavored gelatin

1 (12 oz) can Artificially sweetened
Strawberry soda pop

2¼ cups unsweetened strawberries

Artificial sweetener to = 1 tblsp sugar or
to taste

****

IN SAUCEPAN sprinkle gelatin over soda pop.

ADD strawberries and cook 10 minutes **slow**.

ADD SWEETENER and beat to smooth.

APPROXIMATE EXCHANGE - 1 tsp = trace fruit

SALADS

FRUIT COTTAGE CHEESE SALAD

1 cup unsweetened crushed pineapple
2 small bananas
1/2 cup 2% cottage cheese
10 large cherries, unsweetened canned.

****

DRAIN pineapple and mix with cottage cheese.

CHOP fine banana and cherries.

ADD to cottage cheese.

LINE 6 salad bowls with shredded lettuce.

DIVIDE cottage cheese mixture in bowls.

SPRINKLE with cinnamon.

SERVE immediately.

APPROXIMATE EXCHANGE: 1 serving =

1-1/3 fruit - 1/3 lean meat

COCONUT FRUIT SALAD

2 small apples
2 small bananas
2 tblsp unsweetened flaked coconut
18 small walnuts, chopped
1 tsp grated orange rind
1/2 tsp cinnamon

****

PEEL and chop apples and bananas.

MIX together apples, bananas, rind, coconut, nuts and cinnamon.

SERVE plain or with little whipped cream.

APPROXIMATE EXCHANGE: 1/4 of recipe =

1-1/2 fruit - trace bread - 1 fat + any whip cream used if desired.

PEAR AVOCADO SALAD

3 small pears
1 small apple
2 small oranges
1 avocado (4" in diameter)
1/4 cup orange juice

****

PEEL and chop fine the pears, apple and
oranges.

MIX all together.

IN BLENDER combine peeled chopped avocado
and orange juice and blend slow until
it is like whip cream.

POUR over fruit.

SERVE IMMEDIATELY.

APPROXIMATE EXCHANGE: 1/6 of recipe =

1 fruit - 1-1/3 fat

APPLE BANANA SALAD

2 small apples, finely chopped
1 small banana, chopped
1 tblsp unsweetened coconut
1 tblsp raisins, chopped
9 small walnuts, chopped
1/2 tsp cinnamon (or more if desired)
2 tblsp whipping cream,

****

COMBINE apples, banana, raisins, coconut, and walnuts.

WHIP the cream and add cinnamon to taste.

FOLD cream into fruit.

SERVE on lettuce leaves

EXCHANGE: Complete recipe =

1/5 bread - 4-1/2 fruit - 3-3/4 fat

Other fruit may be added if desired;
such as cantaloupe, honeydew, pineapple
and oranges.

Be sure to add exchanges accordingly
for fruits added or omitted.

PINEAPPLE DATE SALAD

3 cups crushed, drained unsweet pineapple
12 dates, Soak 5 minutes, Drain & chop
2 small bananas
2 cups small green grapes, chopped
18 small walnuts, chopped

****

DRAIN pineapple well; Soak dates in hot water 5 minutes and drain well then chop up small.

CHOP bananas, grapes and nuts.

MIX all ingredients together; Chill.

SERVE on lettuce leaves with coconut dressing.

COCONUT DRESSING

1/4 cup orange juice
1/4 cup pineapple juice
1/4 cup unsweetened coconut

MIX together and toss with fruit.

APPROXIMATE EXCHANGE: 1/12 of recipe -

2 fruit - 1/3 fat - trace bread

MOLDED SALAD

1 envelope unflavored gelatin
1/4 cup cold water
3/4 cup pineapple, crushed, water packed
1/2 cup pineapple juice, Taken from pineapple
1/2 cup orange juice
1 cup fresh frozen cranberries,
    coarse grind while frozen
Artificial sweetener to = 1/3 cup sugar

****

SOFTEN gelatin in water. Drain pineapple &
measure 1/2 cup juice to be used in recipe.

COMBINE cranberries, pineapple and
sweetener & heat to almost boiling.

STIR into gelatin & add juices. POUR into
mold and chill to set.

APPROXIMATE EXCHANGE - 1/8 of recipe =

1/2 fruit

LUNCH SALAD

TOSS TOGETHER - 1/2 cup ground raw carrots,
1 small shredded apple, 1/2 tsp cinnamon,
1 tsp mayonnaise,

APPROXIMATE EXCHANGE - complete recipe =
1 fruit, 1 "B" vegetable, 1 fat

STRAWBERRY JELLO SALAD

1 pkg artificially sweetened strawberry jello
1-3/4 cups boiling water
2 tblsp lemon juice
Artificial sweetener to = 3 tblsp sugar
1 medium fresh peach, chopped fine
1/4 of a small cantaloupe,chopped fine

****

DISSOLVE jello in boiling water.

ADD lemon juice, and sweetener.

CHILL to slightly thickened.

ADD peaches and cantaloupe

CHILL TO SET

APPROXIMATE EXCHANGE - 1/2 of recipe =

1 fruit

COMBINATION SALAD

2 cups cabbage	1/2 cup honeydew
1/2 cup carrots	6 medium prunes
3 small apples	1/2 cup raisins

****

SHRED cabbage and carrots; CHOP fine apples, honeydew melon and prunes.

MIX together with raisins.

POUR dressing over; Toss and serve.

DRESSING

IN BLENDER MIX: 1 small banana, chopped - 1 tblsp mayonnaise - 2 tblsp lemon juice - 2 tblsp water.

BLEND to make dressing desired consistency adding more water if needed.

APPROXIMATE EXCHANGE: 1/6 of recipe =

2 fruit - 2/3 "B" Vegetable - 1/2 fat

CABBAGE CARROT SALAD

3/4 cup cabbage	4 tblsp celery
1/2 cup carrots	1/4 tsp celery seeds

1 pkg artificially sweetened orange jello
2 cups boiling water

****

DISSOLVE jello in water. CHILL to slightly
thickened.

CHOP cabbage, & celery fine

SHRED carrots.

ADD vegetables to jello. ADD celery seeds.

CHILL to thick and set.

SERVE on lettuce leaves.

APPROXIMATE EXCHANGE - 1/3 of recipe =

1 vegetable from list #2 or (B list)

CHICKEN SALAD

9 oz cooked chicken (about 1-1/2 cups)
2 small apples
1/4 cup celery
1/4 cup raisins
2 tsp lemon juice
1/4 cup mayonnaise

****

DICE chicken, apples and celery.

MIX together and add raisins.

CHILL

MIX lemon juice and mayonnaise.

POUR over salad and toss.

LINE 4 salad bowls with shredded lettuce
and divide salad in each.

APPROXIMATE EXCHANGE: 1/4 recipe =

2-1/4 lean meat - 1 fruit - 3 fat

COLESLAW

1 cup cabbage shredded
1/2 cup unsweet, crushed, pineapple, drain
1 small banana
1 small apple
2 tblsp mayonnaise
3 tblsp pineapple juice

****

MIX together cabbage, pineapple,
chopped banana and chopped apple.

MIX together mayonnaise and pineapple
juice.

POUR over salad; Toss lightly and chill.

MAKES 4 servings

APPROXIMATE EXCHANGE:

1 serving = 1 fruit, 1/2 #2 vegetable -
1-1/2 fat

FROZEN FRUIT

GENERAL DIRECTIONS: Prepare fruit as you would for freezing. MIX solution.

FILL freezing containers 1/3 full of solution.

ADD fruit to 1/2 inch of tops & add more solution to just cover fruit. COVER & FREEZE.

BEST if not completely thawed when served.

STORE in refrigerator after opening & use quickly.

****

APPLES or PEACHES - Prepare as for canning.

SOLUTION: 2 cups cold water, ½ tsp ascorbic acid, Liquid sweetener to = 1/3 cup sugar.

****

BLUEBERRIES - Wash & clean & drain.

SOLUTION: 2 cups cold water, Liquid sweetener to = 1/3 cup sugar.

****

STRAWBERRIES - WASH & clean & drain.

TOSS with sweetener solution - Fill freezing containers & freeze.

SOLUTION: 1/3 cup cold water, 2 tblsp unsweetened Orange juice, Liquid sweetener to = 1/3 cup sugar.

HOW TO ORDER ADDITIONAL COPIES
OF THE
"SUGARLESS COOKBOOK"

FOLLOW PRICES BELOW FOR AMOUNT OF BOOKS WANTED.

SEND CHECK OR MONEY ORDER ALONG WITH YOUR MAILING ADDRESS TO:

ADDIE'S RECIPE BOX
DRAWER 5426-SL80
EUGENE, OREGON 97405

1 BOOK $4.95 Plus .70¢ postage = $5.65

2 BOOKS $9.99 POSTAGE PAID

3 BOOKS $14.50 POSTAGE PAID

6 BOOKS $28.00 POSTAGE PAID

Volume prices available to Bookstores, Fundraisers and dealers upon request.